Ludwig van Beethoven

COMPLETE BAGATELLES
for Piano

DOVER PUBLICATIONS, INC.
Mineola, New York

Bibliographical Note

This Dover edition, first published in 2008, is a compilation of works excerpted from an early authoritative edition, and from *Bagatelles, Rondos and Other Shorter Works for Piano,* published in 1987 by Dover Publications, Inc. This in turn was based on "Serie 18. Kleinere Stücke für das Pianoforte" from *Ludwig van Beethoven's Werke. Vollständige kritisch durchgesehene überall berechtigte Ausgabe. Mit Genehmigung aller Originalverleger,* as originally published by Breitkopf & Härtel, Leipzig (complete set, 1862–1865).

The publisher gratefully acknowledges the cooperation of the Paul Klapper Library, Queens College, New York City, for the loan of material reprinted in this volume.

International Standard Book Number
ISBN-13: 978-0-486-46613-2
ISBN-10: 0-486-46613-2

Manufactured in the United States of America
Dover Publications, Inc., 31 East 2nd Street, Mineola, N.Y. 11501

CONTENTS

COMPLETE BAGATELLES
for Piano

SEVEN BAGATELLES

Op. 33

Andante grazioso, quasi allegretto.

4

SCHERZO.

Allegro.

N° 2.

Trio.

Allegretto.

N.º 3.

Nº 4.

Allegro ma non troppo.

Nº 5.

16

18

ELEVEN BAGATELLES

OP. 119

No. 2.

Andante con moto.

à l'Allemande

N.º 3.

Coda.

Da capo fin al segno 𝄋
ed allora la Coda.

Andante cantabile.

N.º 4.

28

Nº 7.

Moderato cantabile.

N°. 8.

molto legato

Vivace moderato.

N°. 9.

Six Bagatelles

Op. 126

32

Andante.
Cantabile e grazioso.

Nº 3.

BAGATELLE
"Für Elise"
WoO 59

BAGATELLE
WoO 56

BAGATELLE
WoO 52